For B.
1 thanke
one
'Brian'

YESTERDAY'S
CARDIFF

Brian Lee

BRIAN LEE

SUTTON PUBLISHING

Sutton Publishing Limited
Phoenix Mill · Thrupp · Stroud
Gloucestershire · GL5 2BU

First published 2007

Title page photograph: A Cardiff bus dating
from 1922. *(B. Warrington)*

British Library Cataloguing in Publication Data
A catalogue record for this book is available from the
British Library.

ISBN 978-07509-4616-2

Typeset in 10.5/13.5 Photina.
Typesetting and origination by
Sutton Publishing Limited.
Printed and bound in England.

Also available from Sutton Publishing

Cardiff's Vanished Docklands

ISBN 978-07509-4424-3

Brian Lee, 2006

For Margaret O'Reilly of the *South Wales Echo*

'Nothing evokes nostalgia quite like an old photograph.
Suddenly the past comes alive before our eyes as we once again
look at long-forgotten faces and places.'

Matthew Williams, curator of Cardiff Castle, 1998

CONTENTS

ACKNOWLEDGEMENTS

I would like to thank all those people who provided me with the photographs for this book. Thanks are also due to Tony Woolway, chief librarian at the *Western Mail & Echo*, and to his colleagues Edwina Turner and Rob Mager for their assistance. I also need to acknowledge the help of Katrina Coopey and her staff at Cardiff Central Library Local Studies Department for their help over the years. As I am planning to compile a second selection for *Yesterday's Cardiff*, I would like to hear from readers who may have photographs for possible inclusion. I can be contacted by telephone on 02920736438 or care of my publishers. Finally, my grateful thanks to all those at Sutton Publishing for assisting me in the production of this book.

INTRODUCTION

We begin our walk down Cardiff's memory lane with a look at Cardiff Castle and the civic centre. The famous castle, situated right in the heart of the capital city of Wales, was at first, nearly 2,000 years ago, a Roman fort, an eight-acre stronghold standing on the banks of the River Taff. It was rebuilt two centuries later with 10ft walls, part of which still stand today.

In 1947 the Marquess of Bute presented Cardiff Castle and Bute Park to the citizens of Cardiff and ever since the castle has been a great tourist attraction. The Romans built a fortress on the site in 76 AD and this was discovered in 1889 when Lord Bute ordered excavations to be carried out.

Around 1093 the Norman Robert Fitzhamon invaded the old Welsh kingdom and established himself at Cardiff, building a castle on the site of the old Roman fort.

During the excavations of 1922/3 a perfect example of a Roman wall was discovered extending 270ft in length from the Castle Street entrance. Within the castle's ground is The Keep, an original mound 40ft high. It is thought by some that this mound is the work of Danes who had a settlement in the area during the tenth and eleventh centuries. However, it is more likely the work of the Normans.

Of all the statues in the civic centre, the equestrian one of the 1st Viscount Lord Tredegar, in the uniform of the 17th lancers, in front of the City Hall is probably the best known. It is most unusual in that it was erected in 1909 when he was still alive and in his presence. The horse, Sir Briggs, which carried Lord Tredegar – Captain Godfrey Charles Morgan – in the historic ill-fated Charge of the Light Brigade at Balaclava in 1854 sustained a sabre cut to one of his ears.

In Gorsedd Gardens can be found the life-size statues of John Cory, coal owner and philanthropist, and Lord Ninian Stuart, grandson of the 2nd Marquess of Bute, MP for Cardiff, who was killed in action at Loos in 1915 during the First World War. These statues, like the equestrian one, were executed by the eminent Cardiff sculptor Sir William Goscombe John.

The South African War memorial between the Law Courts and the City Hall was erected in memory of the 200 soldiers killed serving in Welsh regiments. While in Alexandra Gardens can be seen the statues of Henry Austin Bruce. The first Lord Aberdare, he was President of the University of Wales. The magnificent Welsh National War Memorial, also in Alexandra Gardens, was unveiled by Edward, Prince of Wales in 1928. The main features of this Romanesque Portland stone memorial are the three bronze statues of a sailor, soldier and airman. Outside the Law Courts stands the statue of Judge Gwilym Williams of Miskin whose 'crowning glory' was 'his ardent love for his nation – its tradition, its people, its music, its poetry, its language, its life, which he touched with every facet', while in Friary Gardens is the monument to John Patrick Crichton Stuart, 3rd Marquess of Bute who, like his father, was one of the modern builders of Cardiff. This was unveiled by his son on 15 October 1930.

There are other statues in the civic centre, including one of Lloyd George erected in Gorsedd Gardens in 1960. Most impressive of the civic centre buildings is the City Hall with its great tall clock tower and dome surmounted by a fiery Welsh dragon. Officially opened in 1906, it is indeed a splendid building with a magnificent circular council chamber and a marble hall with striking statues of the Heroes of Wales. The Law Courts, the National Museum of Wales, Cardiff University and the old Welsh National Board of Health buildings are other places of interest we visit in chapter one, along with the New Theatre which celebrated its centenary in 2006 and has served its patrons well over the years staging musicals, operas, dramatic plays, pantomime, variety shows and circus. You name it the 'New' has staged it. Many great stars have trod its boards and long may they continue to do so.

In chapter two, City Centre Scenes, we see the ever-changing face of Cardiff including once-familiar shops such as Littlewoods, Allders, David Morgan and Greenfields which have disappeared to make to make way for new ones. Warehouses and the open-air market on Mill Lane is now the site of the Marriott Hotel.

We journey back to 1909 in chapter three to visit the National Pageant of Wales held in Sophia Gardens and which was probably the biggest event staged in Cardiff since the Cardiff Fine Art, Industrial and Maritime Exhibition of 1896. Such was the pageant's popularity that more than 60,000 schoolchildren had booked seats at the dress rehearsals three weeks before it opened. Hundreds of ladies in Cardiff voluntarily lent their services in assisting to make the costumes for the 5,000 performers and the 1,200 children who took part.

The *Western Mail & Echo* is the subject of chapter four which includes some fascinating pictures of the building of Thomson House where both the *Western Mail*, the national daily morning newspaper of Wales, and the *South Wales Echo* are produced. Thomson House was built in the area of Cardiff known as Temperance Town and built partly on the former bed of the River Taff when it once flowed through what is now Westgate Street.

In chapter five we pay a visit to the much-lamented Lears Bookshop and meet some of the famous authors who had signings there, including Emlyn Williams, Barry John, Gareth Davies and Cardiff's own author/publisher Stewart Williams.

The much-loved David Morgan family store is remembered in chapter six as well as other vanished shops and businesses including Seccombes, Paige, and Jupps sweet factory in Whitchurch.

We pay tribute to Cardiff's fire-fighters in chapter seven with some dramatic fire-fighting pictures, and we are reminded that our firemen were once based in Westgate Street until the building was demolished in 1973 to make way for a multi-storey car park.

The various forms of transport that Cardiffians have made use of over the years are featured in chapter eight, from horse and carriages to trams and trolleybuses.

Some memorable moments are recaptured in chapter nine, including the retirements of *Western Mail & Echo* compositors whom the author worked alongside for many years. We also see a young Shirley Bassey signing autographs and Harry Secombe and Ivor Emmanuel in the Kings Cross pub in Canton.

Greyhound racing at the old Cardiff Arms Park, charabanc outings, visits to Roath Park and Barry Island are just some of the subjects covered in chapter ten, Leisure Time, before moving on to chapter eleven, Cardiff at War, in which we visit bomb-damaged streets and churches and take part in some of the after-war celebrations.

We return to our schooldays for chapter twelve, and you, or your parents or grandparents may even be one of those children in the school photographs that are featured.

Finally, we end our journey down Cardiff's memory lane with chapter thirteen, Sporting Moments. We attend the opening and closing ceremony of the 1958 sixth British Empire and Commonwealth Games at the Cardiff Arms Park, we go horseracing at Ely Racecourse, which opened in 1855 and closed in 1939, and we take a trip to a packed Maindy Stadium for the Welsh Games and other sporting events.

1

Civic Centre

The Imperial Fruit Show was held in Cardiff between 25 October and 2 November 1935, and this postcard inviting 'your friends to Cardiff . . . The most beautiful city in Wales' was sent to Mrs W.H. Slade of No. 2 Northcote Street, Stapleton Road, Bristol. (*Author's Collection*)

Cardiff Castle's octagonal Chaucer Tower, seen here in about 1920, was the first part of the modern castle to be built by Richard Beauchamp, Earl of Warwick and Lord of Glamorgan between 1425 and 1430. *(Author's Collection)*

The mound upon which the castle keep stands is thought to be of Norman origin, but Danes had a settlement in the area in the tenth and eleventh centuries. The City Hall can be seen in the background, *c.* 1920. *(Ernest T. Bush)*

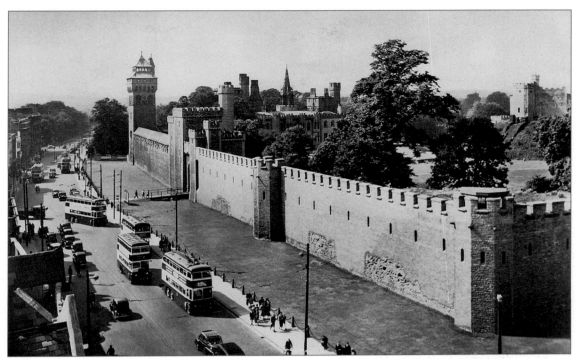

In the centre can be seen the south wing of the castle, rebuilt by architect William Burgess for the third Marquis of Bute in 1893. The trolleybuses to the left of the picture, seen here in about 1958, ran in Cardiff between 1942 and 1970. (*Author's Collection*)

There wasn't much traffic about when this picture of the castle and Duke Street was taken by H.T. Beach in the 1920s. (*Author's Collection*)

This statue of Judge Gwilym Williams (1839–1906), sculpted by Cardiff's William Goscombe John, stands outside the Law Courts, *c.* 1920. *(Author's Collection)*

Designed by Lanchester, Stewart and Rickards, the two-storey Law Courts were completed in 1904, *c.* 1950. *(Author's Collection)*

Cardiff's most impressive building with its magnificent clock tower is the City Hall, opened in 1906. The dome is surmounted by a Welsh dragon and the equestrian statue is that of Lord Tredegar and his famous charger Sir Briggs, *c.* 1920. *(W.H.S. & Strand)*

The stone for the National Museum of Wales was laid in 1912, but owing to the First World War the main block and western galleries were not opened until 1927 – around the time this picture was taken. *(Author's Collection)*

Opened in Cathays Park as the Welsh National Board of Health building in 1938 it is now the Welsh Office and has been extended, *c.* 1938. *(Author's Collection)*

A rare shot of the University of Wales in Cathays Park. The west wing was opened in 1909 and the rest of the building between 1912 and 1962. This picture for this postcard was taken in about 1924. *(Author's Collection)*

In the centre of Alexandra Gardens stands the National War Memorial of Wales, unveiled by Edward, Prince of Wales in June 1928. This British Manufacture postcard appears to have been taken shortly after the unveiling. *(Author's Collection)*

The sculptured groups at either end of the Glamorgan County Hall building represent navigation and mining, *c.* 1954. As a young lad, the author was told off for playing on the statues! *(Author's Collection)*

The South African War Memorial in Cathays Park, seen here in about 1920, was erected in memory of around 200 soldiers who died serving in Welsh regiments. It is the work of sculptor Albert Toft. *(Ernest T. Bush)*

The New Theatre in Park Place, which celebrated its centenary in December 2006, has served its patrons well with a rich and varied assortment of entertainment from pantomime to opera, *c.* 1920. *(Ernest T. Bush)*

2

City Centre Scenes

Council workmen in the Mill Lane and Custom House Street area preparing for the new one-way system, May 1968. The Marriott Hotel now stands on the site of the open-air market, to the left of the picture. *(Western Mail & Echo)*

Work on the Marriott Hotel was in progress when this photograph was taken by Gerald May in May 1985. The sign for the entrance to the Royal Arcade, opened in 1858, can be seen to the right of the picture. *(Gerald May)*

The statue of John Batchelor in the centre of the picture was unveiled in 1886. It has been moved on several occasions since. The building in the background is the popular David Morgan family store which closed in 2005 after 125 years' unrivalled service to shoppers, *c.* 1910. *(Author's Collection)*

These two pictures taken from the roof of the David Morgan family store in 1978 shows the site of the Heron Development. The building to the left is the former South Wales Electricity showrooms. It opened in 1901 as The New Wholesale Fish, Poultry, Bird, Game, Fruit and Vegetable Market and was built on the site of the old St John's Infant School. The building, now Habitat, adjoined the Glamorganshire Canal on its eastern side. St David's Cathedral can be seen in the background. *(Author's Collection)*

Another part of the city centre which is undergoing redevelopment again is St David's Centre, which was opened in 1982 and is seen here in May 1985. *(Gerald May)*

Developers wanted to convert Rapport warehouse in Bridge Street into a multi-million-pound dance bar, restaurant, cocktail bar, function suite and café in 1988, but it is still being used as a warehouse. *(Western Mail & Echo)*

British Home Stores moved across the road from their home of thirty years on the corner of Queen Street and Priory Street to larger premises at the former Woolworth store in 1988. It was in 1955 that BHS, which began in London in 1929, opened in Cardiff on the site of the old Carlton Restaurant which was damaged by German bombs in the Second World War. This picture was taken in 1985. *(Western Mail & Echo)*

Littlewoods in Queen Street closed in 1998 and was taken over by Marks & Spencer, seen here in about 1990. It is currently a branch of Next. The first letterbox in Cardiff was erected in Queen Street, then known as Crockherbtown, in 1855. Crockherbtown was renamed Queen Street in 1886. *(Western Mail & Echo)*

A busy Queen Street scene and another vanished store is Allders, 1980. There is a plaque on the wall on the extreme right of this picture which commemorates the medieval gateway into the town from the east. *(Western Mail & Echo)*

There was a closing down sale at Greenfields in Queen Street when this picture was taken in November 1984. The other buildings in the picture retained their upper structure Victorian frontages. Clinton Cards is now situated on the site. *(Western Mail & Echo)*

Older Cardiffians will remember the popular Dutch Café in Queen Street which, along with Halfords, was demolished in the late 1980s to make way for the Queens West shopping centre. The tiles showing four Dutch men were saved and were incorporated in the wall of the new building in Station Terrace, March 1987. *(Western Mail & Echo)*

The Pavilion Cinema in St Mary Street opened in 1876 as a theatre called the Philharmonic Hall. It has also been known as Stoll's Panopticon (1882) and the Pavilion (1916). Between 1970 and 1994 it was known as the Gala Cascade Bingo & Social Club. This picture shows one of the street decorations for the 1964 Cardiff Shopping Festival. *(Western Mail & Echo)*

There have been many changes to Cardiff Prison since this picture was taken in September 1956. The last man to be hanged in the prison was Mahmoud Mattan in 1952. His family always maintained his innocence and in 1998 his conviction was set aside. *(Western Mail & Echo)*

This was how the rear of Charles Street looked from Frederick Street in May 1971. Charles Street was named after Charles Vachell who played a big part in the implementation of the Public Health Act (1848). He was elected Mayor on two occasions (1849 and 1855). The first mention of Charles Street appears in Piggot's Street Directory of 1835. *(Western Mail & Echo)*

3

The Pageant of Wales

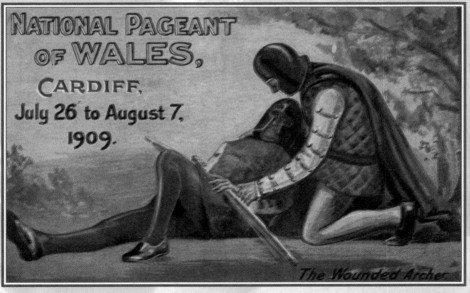

In 1909, 175,000 spectators attended the National Pageant of Wales in Sophia Gardens. It depicted the history of Wales from the first century to Henry VIII's Act of Union. *(Author's Collection)*

The opening scene. The most noble the Marchioness of Bute (centre) assumed the character of 'Dame Wales'. (*Author's Collection*)

Mr Victor Wiltshire as King Henry V at Agincourt. (*Author's Collection*)

The storming of Cardiff Castle by the
Welsh clansman Ivor Bach, 1158. Some
500 prominent football players took part
in this episode. (*Author's Collection*)

Miss Nest Williams, of St Donat's Castle,
as Queen of Gruffydd Ap Llywelyn.
(*Author's Collection*)

Mr Godfrey Williams as Owen Tudor and the Hon. Mrs Godfrey Williams as Queen Catherine. *(Author's Collection)*

Lady Ninian Crichton Stuart as Glamorgan. *(Author's Collection)*

Harry Tudor (Henry VI) crowned on the field after the battle of Bosworth on 22 August 1485. *(Author's Collection)*

Declaration of War to Caradoc against the Romans, 50 AD. *(Author's Collection)*

Vortigern and Cunedda, 449 AD. Emperor
Vortigern was played by Mr W. Milward of
Claude Road, Cardiff, and King Cunedda by
Mr E. Thomas of Inverness Place, Cardiff.
(*Author's Collection*)

The most noble the Marchioness of Bute
'Dame Wales'. (*Author's Collection*)

The famous Welsh bard Davydd ap Gwilym and the twenty fair damsels he immortalised dancing on the Pageant Field. Davydd ap Gwilym was played by Mr Richard Harris of Clare Road, Cardiff. *(Author's Collection)*

According to the postcard this is Viscount Lord Tredegar as Owen Glyndwr, Prince of Wales. But it is in fact Lord Mostyn re-enacting the part of his great ancestor, Richard ap Howel of Mostyn, to whom Henry VII the first of the Tudors presented his battle sword after the great victory of Bosworth. *(Author's Collection)*

Mr Ernest George Cove as Fluellen.
(Author's Collection)

Thousands of Cardiff schoolchildren took
part in the closing ceremony and they
joined up to form a map of Wales.
(Author's Collection)

4

Western Mail & Echo

The Park Street site on which the offices of the *Western Mail & Echo* Thomson House building was erected, 1957. Today the newspapers are printed in the Cardiff Bay area but all the editorial work is still done in Thomson House. (*Western Mail & Echo*)

The foundations for the building were built partly on the former bed of the River Taff. The author worked as a stereotyper on the *Western Mail* for eighteen years and the *South Wales Echo* for ten years in the old and new buildings, February 1957. *(Western Mail & Echo)*

A total of 600 tons of steel, 8,000 tons of concrete and 500,000 bricks were used to construct the new building, seen here in October 1958. *(Western Mail & Echo)*

The architects for the new building were Ellis, Clarke and Gallannaugh and the main contractors were John Morgan (Cardiff) Ltd. Seen here in 1960, the building was officially opened by Lord Thomson on 20 June 1961. (*Western Mail & Echo*)

This was how the Park Street side of Thomson House looked in 1959. Park Street was so named because of its close proximity to the Cardiff Arms Park. (*Western Mail & Echo*)

A rear view of the building showing cars parked in Scott Road, 1960. *(Western Mail & Echo)*

On the move! From left to right, compositors Fred Suller, Malcolm Hope, Wyndham Davies and Dave Pedrick help with the move to the new building in 1960. The old building on the corner of St Mary Street and Westgate Street was just a matter of yards away. Who is the chap in the background? *(Western Mail & Echo)*

This is heavier than I thought! Wyndham Davies and Dave Pedrick give a helping hand, 1960. (*Western Mail & Echo*)

This picture was taken in the old building on the corner of St Mary Street and Westgate Street in about 1955. It shows, from left to right, Idwal Morgan, George Murphy and Cliff Davies working on the stone, while seated at their linotype machines are Reg Rees and Jack Chamberlain (right). (*Western Mail & Echo*)

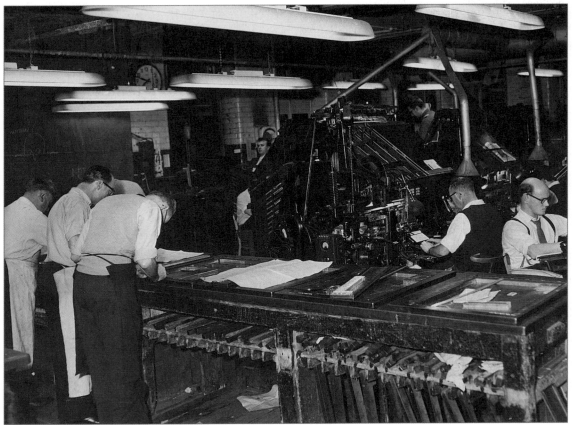

The jobbing section of the composing room in the new building, 1961. (*Western Mail & Echo*)

Malcolm Roles (left) and Geoffrey North are lifted shoulder high after the banging out ceremony by their journeymen workmates having completing their apprenticeships, March 1979. (*Western Mail & Echo*)

Compositors Alan Jones (first on the left) and Gerard Kingston assist stereotyper Reg Potter to put a page on the mangle. They are being watched by overseer Len Smith on his final day of work, 1969. (*Western Mail & Echo*)

The end of an era. On 2 February 1980 the last hot metal page was sent to the press and *South Wales Echo* editor Geoff Rich was invited to complete the page. Fred Simmons, wearing spectacles, is looking over his shoulder. An apron was presented to Geoff by Gerard Kingston and he took it home to his wife Sybil with strict instructions not to wash it! (*Western Mail & Echo*)

Computer keyboard room, June 1980. When the new technology was introduced, Doug Fisher (right) had the responsibility of training his colleagues to use the computers. *(Western Mail & Echo)*

Doug Fisher (left) with managing director David Thomas (centre) and Lord Thomson. Composing room overseer Brian Codd, partially obscured on the extreme right of the picture, sadly died in 2006. *(Western Mail & Echo)*

5

Lears Bookshop

Author/publisher Stewart Williams (centre) is seen shaking hands with Jim Edmunds, managing director of Lears Bookshop in St Mary Street, at the launch of his book *Vintage Buses and Trams in South Wales* in April 1975. The gentleman on the left of the picture is Gerry Thomas who worked for the *Western Mail & Echo*. Lears bookshop originated as an evangelical bookshop at No. 17 Royal Arcade in 1887. Blackwells bought the business in the late 1980s and it closed its doors in May 2002.
(Jim Edmunds)

Jim Edmunds gives a final shake of the hand to Stewart Williams whose magnificent series of thirty-six *Cardiff Yesterday* books inspired the author. The historic horse-drawn coach had been rebuilt in 1968 by E. Andrews & Son of Cardiff. *(Jim Edmunds)*

The author Brian Lee (left) listens intently to what J.A. Brooks, author of *Railway Ghosts*, has to say at one of Lears popular book launches in 1985. *(Jim Edmunds)*

In 1978 the famed rugby scrum-half Gareth Edwards signed copies of his book in Lears bookshop. His 53 caps for Wales, 13 as captain, was a record until it was beaten by J.P.R. Williams in 1981. *(Jim Edmunds)*

Author Bobby Freeman (right) at the launch of her book *First Catch Your Peacock*. It seems R.E. 'Wyn' Thomas, the managing director, had already caught his! *(Jim Edmunds)*

Leighton Rees (left), winner of the first world professional darts championship in 1978, at the launch of his book *Leighton Rees On Darts* in October 1979. *(Jim Edmunds)*

Television personalities Griff Rhys-Jones and Mel Smith show off their book *The Smith and Jones World Atlas* in the early 1980s. *(Jim Edmunds)*

Famous Welsh actor and author Emlyn Williams (1905–87) posed for this picture at the launch of his book *Headlong* in 1980. *(Jim Edmunds)*

BBC television wildlife expert David Attenborough signing copies of his book *Life on Earth* in November 1979. *(Jim Edmunds)*

A familiar face with thousands of television viewers is that of Frank Muir, 23 October 1979. *(Jim Edmunds)*

Another Welsh rugby legend who had his book launch at Lears was Phil Bennett. He set a number of scoring records during his international career and played for Llanelli, the Barbarians and the British Lions. He was awarded the OBE in 1978 and this picture was taken a year later. *(Jim Edmunds)*

Joint authors rugby writer John Reason (left) and Carwyn James signing copies of their book *The World of Rugby* in 1979. Carwyn James, a former Welsh International, coached the British Lions team in New Zealand in 1971. He died in Amsterdam in 1983. *(Jim Edmunds)*

Carmarthen-born Gerald Davies who at one time shared with Gareth Edwards the Welsh record for scoring the most international tries. In 1971, he helped Wales to the Grand Slam and when he retired became rugby correspondent of *The Times*, *c*. 1979. (*Jim Edmunds*)

Dubbed 'The King' Barry John set numerous scoring records which he would almost certainly have bettered had he not retired from the game at the early age of twenty-seven. He was partnered by Gareth Edwards in all but two of his twenty-five games for Wales. He is seen signing copies of his book *Barry John's World of Rugby* in November 1979. (*Jim Edmunds*)

6

Shops & Businesses

James Howell's departmental store in St Mary Street. Mr Howell opened a store on
The Hayes in 1865 and it became one of the oldest and largest stores in Cardiff.
The building seen to the right of the picture was sold to House of Fraser in 1972.
(Author's Collection)

The popular Seccombes store in Queen Street which closed in 1977. Note the date on the top of the building: 1885. Their motto read 'Seccombes Of Cardiff Where Quality Counts', *c.* 1975. *(Derek Carder)*

This picture shows some of the bedrooms of the Park Hotel which faces on to Queen Street, *c.* 1980. The Park Hotel, now part of the Thistle group, was built in French Renaissance style in 1885. The Nationwide Building society has now moved to much bigger premises in Queen Street. *(Derek Carder)*

Paige, the ladies' fashion shop, was situated between Palmer the gentlemen's outfitters and Van Allan in Queen Street. Van Allan was adjacent to the Midland Bank building, now HSBC, *c.* 1980. *(Derek Carder)*

True-Form shoe shop stood on the corner of Queen Street and Frederick Street. Queen Street was once known as Crockherbtown and in 1862 many of the old buildings were demolished when the street was widened, *c.* 1980. *(Derek Carder)*

The Refuge Assurance Co. Ltd office was on the corner of Queen Street and St John Street, popularly known as St John's Square. The entrance to High Street Arcade can be seen to the right of the picture, *c.* 1980. *(Derek Carder)*

Mothercare, which was situated on the corner of Queen Street and Charles Street. The building on the right is Marks & Spencer and on the same side can be seen St David's Roman Catholic Cathedral, *c.* 1980. *(David Carder)*

The Odeon cinema in Queen Street first opened as the Imperial Picture Palace in 1911 and became the Odeon in 1936. Like the adjacent Wimpy Bar it has since disappeared. *c.* 1980. *(Derek Carder)*

The Principality Building Society, on the left of the picture, and Lloyds, now Lloyds TSB, are still in Queen Street but Burtons, on the right, is no more, *c.* 1980. *(Derek Carder)*

Renewing the roof with Welsh slate at Cardiff Castle are, from right to left, Howard Gill snr, Howard Gill jnr, Nigel Gill and David Marshall. The ornate clock tower was built between 1867 and 1872. This picture was taken on 15 September 1980. *(Nigel Gill)*

A well-known Cardiff landmark was the much-loved David Morgan family store which stood on The Hayes from 1879 to 2005. This photograph was probably taken in the early 1970s. *(Author's Collection)*

There was a good selection of chocolates (right of picture) on display when this picture was taken in David Morgan's ground-floor department in the 1970s. *(Author's Collection)*

Another David Morgan ground-floor picture believed to have been taken in the 1970s. The gentleman appears to be carrying out a survey of the area. *(Author's Collection)*

This Saturday Sellouts picture was taken on the second floor of the building, *c.* 1970. Why the Leicester City FC gear is on sale in a Cardiff store remains a mystery! *(Author's Collection)*

The entrance to the lingerie department, 1999. *(Author's Collection)*

David Morgan lingerie department staff, from left to right: Ann Llewellyn, Joan Dale, Mary Brown, Sharon Amey, Maureen Fitzgibbon, Cheryl Durante and Julie Carpenter, 1999. *(Author's Collection)*

Fashion shows were regularly held in David Morgan's. Unfortunately, the names of these three glamorous ladies are unknown, *c.* 1990. *(Author's Collection)*

David Morgan fashion show, *c.* 1990.
'Where did she get that hat?'
(*Author's Collection*)

David Morgan fashion show, *c.* 1990.
This smart outfit would certainly not look
out of place at Royal Ascot today.
(*Author's Collection*)

Some older Cardiffians may remember the family-run Jupps Sweets factory in Whitchurch which traded between 1920 and 1966. The gentleman on the right in the picture below is Mr Edward Jupp, *c.* 1950. *(Mrs Jennifer Leonard, née Jupp)*

7

Cardiff's Fire-fighters

The Cardiff City Fire Service team which won the 1951 national first-aid competition.
(Derek Carder)

Station officer Derek Carder, communications officer (right) and fireman Lennard Wheeler pictured in the new Adam Street fire headquarters of the South Glamorgan fire service's new mobile incident control unit, November 1978. *(Derek Carder)*

Station officer Derek Carder is pictured outside the South Glamorgan Fire Service incident control room, December 1978. *(Derek Carder)*

South Glamorgan Fire Service members in the first computerised control room in Adam Street, 1985. *(Derek Carder)*

HRH the Prince of Wales paid a visit to the South Glamorgan County Council emergency control room set up in County Headquarters, Newport Road, in 1982. *(Derek Carder)*

A serious fire occurred at the premises of Meggitt and Jones' timber yard in the docklands area on 11 August 1962. *(Derek Carder)*

Fireman Derek Carder surveys the damage done to a road tanker that caught fire in Cardiff Docks in November 1988. *(Derek Carder)*

In the 1970s, an old Dennis fire engine was used by the Cardiff Fire Brigade as a means of collecting money for charity. *(Derek Carder)*

There were several serious fires in Cardiff during the 1960s and this one occurred at J. & R. Griffiths Ltd, West Canal Wharf on 8 March 1963. In another, five people were killed when a two-storey dwelling house in North William Street caught fire. These pictures show how the fire-fighters dealt with them. *(Derek Carder)*

Gloria Haycock (née Dowding) in 1968 (right), who married Fireman Colin Haycock (below) and went on to become an Assistant Divisional Officer. She was the first female fire control operator to be appointed, as prior to then firemen undertook duties in the control room as part of their official fire duties.
(Derek Carder)

The pilot and three passengers were killed when a light aeroplane crashed in North Road, near Maindy Stadium on 6 May 1959. It took firemen thirty minutes to control the fire. The aircraft had taken off from Sophia Gardens where the Ideal Home Exhibition was being held. (*Derek Carder*)

Clearing up the mess after a house fire are firemen Slackman, Newman and Patterson, *c.* 1964. *(Derek Carder)*

Firemen on a special service call to Fulton, Dunlop & Co. Ltd in the city centre. The fireman at the top of the ladder is dealing with the loose cement brickwork which was a hazard to passers-by, *c.* 1955. *(Derek Carder)*

The six-storey Westgate Street fire station built in Georgian style was opened in 1917. It was demolished in the late 1970s to make way for a multi-storey car park, *c.* 1960. *(Author's Collection)*

Members of the Cardiff Fire Brigade posed for this group picture outside the Westgate Street fire station in 1958. *(Derek Carder)*

Proudly standing in front of the new steam fire engines is superintendent G. Geen who resigned in 1917 after nearly forty-three faithful years' service, 1913. *(Author's Collection)*

On the morning of 16 August 1958 the warehouses on The Hayes caught fire and it took seventeen jets from eight pumps to subdue the fire. The Central Cinema can be seen in the centre of the picture. *(Author's Collection)*

8

Transport

Horse-drawn trams were still in vogue in Cardiff in 1900.
(Author's Collection)

The driver of these two buses was Mr Don Lee who lived at No. 42 Chestnut Road, Fairwater, Cardiff. The top picture was taken in 1922 and the bottom one in 1925. *(B. Warrington)*

A horse-drawn tram passing the turnpike at Penarth Road. Note the hoarding advertising the Empire Theatre in Queen Street, *c. 1909. (Author's Collection)*

There were more horses in Cardiff than cars when this picture was taken in the Pontcanna area in about 1910. *(Author's Collection)*

Electric trams ran throughout Cardiff between 1902 and 1950. This picture shows the last tram which was decorated for the occasion on 20 February 1950. *(Rita Georgyer)*

Trolleybuses first came into service in Cardiff in 1942. This picture shows trolleybus 216 rounding the monument on its approach to St Mary Street, 24 April 1968. *(Mike Street)*

One of the last trolleybuses to be bought by Cardiff Corporation in 1955 passes the civic centre on the new one-way system, 19 April 1968. (*Mike Street*)

Trolleybus 262 turns at Victoria Park terminus, 28 April 1968. (*Mike Street*)

Trolleybuses stopped running in Cardiff on 3 December 1969. However, training continued almost until the end and this one, note the L-plate, is parked at the terminus in Central Square, 24 April 1968.
(Mike Street)

This trolleybus is about to pass under the Taff Railway bridge on Newport Road on its way to the terminus, 26 April 1968. Note the ladies and gentlemen's toilets to the right of the vehicle which, like the buildings to the left of the picture, are long gone. *(Mike Street)*

This South Wales Electricity van, which was used for delivering appliances to customers, is pictured outside their showrooms in Hill Street in April 1990. The building, which was originally a fish market, is now Habitat. *(Mike Street)*

This ex-wartime National Fire Service vehicle was called to a fire in Tudor Street on 17 August 1968. *(Mike Street)*

Parked outside the Thomson House side entrance in Park Street on 26 October 1977 is a Morrison Electricar van – one of ten experimental vehicles bought by the Post Office in 1969. *(Mike Street)*

The *South Wales Echo*'s fleet of vans in 1960, which distributed the paper throughout the land. Sadly, the *Sports Echo* advertised on some of the vans ceased publication in 2005. *(Doug Fisher)*

Parked outside Boots in Queen Street is this Cardiff City Council (Cleansing Division) vehicle which did duty in the city centre, April 1990. *(Mike Street)*

Cardiff City Council (Cleansing Division) Laird Rotopress refuse compactor vehicle on the corner of Park Place and Queen Street, April 1990. This vehicle was sold in 1991 after being bought new in 1985. *(Mike Street)*

Cardiff City Council (City Engineers Department) vehicle used for flushing sewers outside the Central Library in April 1990. The library was demolished in April 2007 to make way for the St David's 2 development. *(Mike Street)*

A British Telecom vehicle which was used for light cabling duties parked in Wood Street, April 1990. *(Mike Street)*

9

Memorable Moments

The former Prime Minister Mr James Callaghan, MP for Cardiff South and Penarth, and Police Inspector Dave Francis share a joke over the route of the Cardiff to London walk, a sponsored event to raise money for community projects in Butetown and the Variety Club of Great Britain, May 1986. Looking on from the left are PC Colin Williams, PC Bob Roberts, Inspector Colin Francis and Lyn James of the Variety Club.
(Western Mail & Echo)

Fourteen-year-old Carolyn Williams of Park Avenue, Whitchurch, Cardiff, was the millionth visitor to the Llanishen Leisure Centre in October 1988. She won two return air tickets to Stuttgart and two nights bed and breakfast courtesy of Holiday Inn. The Lord Mayor of Cardiff, councillor Bill Herbert, joined in the celebrations. (*Western Mail & Echo*)

The Lord Mayor of Cardiff, councillor John Edwards, enjoys a browse through the pages of *Cardiff Yesterday* (volume 2) with author and publisher Stewart Williams. A copy was presented to the Lord Mayor by the author in the City Hall parlour on 3 April 1981. (*Western Mail & Echo*)

Cheque mates. From left to right: Cardiff Bay development chief Barry Lane, carnival committee vice-chairman Steve Khaireh, community affairs consultant Viv Brook and carnival organiser Elvin Blades. A cheque for £2,250 was presented to the festival organisers by the Cardiff Bay Development Corporation in August 1988. The much-loved Viv Brook used to be the South Wales Assistant Chief Constable. *(Western Mail & Echo)*

A young looking and shoeless Shirley Bassey signing autographs for her fans in May 1957. The store is believed to be Victor Freed in Duke Street. *(Western Mail & Echo)*

Lisa Coffey, of Bro Des, Pentyrch, had a swinging time at the Charles Street carnival in July 1986. *(Western Mail & Echo)*

Mrs Florence Cowling from Avon Street, Canton, Cardiff, with singer Ivor Emmanuel at the Kings Castle public house in Canton, *c.* 1950. *(Donald Williams)*

This picture was also taken in the Kings Castle and shows Harry Secombe holding a baby. On the extreme right is Mrs Florence Cowling, *c.* 1950 *(Donald Williams)*

Deputy Lord Mayor, councillor John Smith traversing the climbing wall for charity outside the old Central Library in Working Street, 1988. *(Western Mail & Echo)*

South Wales Echo compositor Ken Jeans retired in February 1983, ending the Jeans family long connection with the *Western Mail & Echo*. Pictured are Dick Sherman, Alec Speed, Alan Jones, Tony Bravey, Brian Codd, Bill Edwards, Fred Simmons, Bryn Devonald, Glyn Coward, Harold Bithell, Jim Morgan, Ben Cox, Mike Bishop and Doug Fisher. *(Doug Fisher)*

Members of the composing room staff at the *South Wales Echo* gather around to give a send off to their colleague Ernie Hope, of York Street, Canton, Cardiff, who retired after nearly forty years' service with the paper. Father of the chapel (shop steward) Ted Roberts presents him with a cheque and a silver goblet from his workmates, 28 July 1977. *(Doug Fisher)*

Managing director David Thomas (left) cracks a joke at the retirement lunch of Ted Roberts (FOC) in October 1979. Also in the picture, from left to right, are Jack Relph, Mr Hudson, Doug Hales, Doug Fisher, Jack Savage, Alec Speed, R. Mitchell, Ken Smith and John Williams. *(Doug Fisher)*

Ted Roberts presenting Dai 'Merthyr' Thompson with a cheque and a tankard on behalf of his workmates on the occasion of his retirement, 21 October 1975. *(Doug Fisher)*

South Wales Echo chief overseer Jack Philips pours himself a drink on his last day at work in 1974. *(Doug Fisher)*

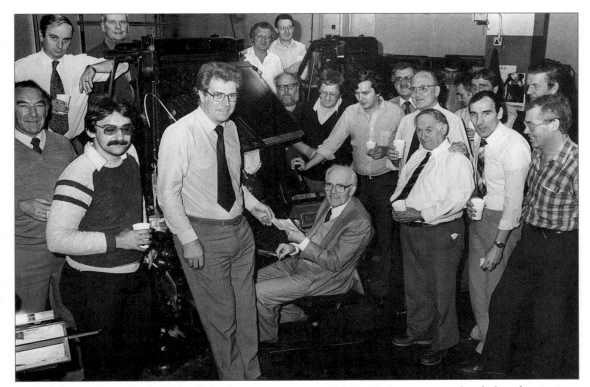

A fond farewell to *South Wales Echo* linotype operator Bobby Parker, seen at his beloved Intertype machine in November 1982. Also in the picture are Ron Howell, Doug Fisher, Reg Potter, Alec Speed (FOC), Gerard Kingston, Ken Jones, Dick Sherman, Brian Codd, George Brunker, Harold Bithnell, Dave Pedrick, Glyn Coward, John Freshney and Dave Griffiths. *(Doug Fisher)*

Three cheers for composing room overseer George Codd (hands together) who retired in May 1971. In the foreground, from left to right, are overseers Ron Bibbings, Jack Philips, Ted Roberts and Jack Bickley. *(Doug Fisher)*

Linotype operator Archie Hine retired after fifty years' service and to mark the occasion he was presented with a stainless steel tea service and cutlery from the National Graphical Association Chapel (day and night members) by Ken Jeans the day father of the chapel. On the extreme left is British featherweight boxing champion Malcolm Collins, May 1970. *(Doug Fisher)*

It's goodbye to the *South Wales Echo*'s Ben Cox (second left) who worked on the Intertype headline machine for many years. Also in the foreground, from left to right, are Brian Codd, Ted Roberts, Trevor Lloyd and Jack Bickley, 28 February 1974. *(Doug Fisher)*

The *Western Mail & Echo*'s first-aid representatives celebrate with a drink after obtaining their first-aid certificates, December 1970. *(Doug Fisher)*

The final computer training class, December 1980. Standing: reader Bill Keenor, Trevor Brunker, Alan Cross, Jeff North and Doug Evans. Seated: Bob Parker and trainer Doug Fisher. *(Doug Fisher)*

Preparing for the last Taff Swim held in Roath Park Lake in 1961. *Western Mail & Echo* workers, from left to right, are stereotyper Stan Parsons and carpenters Tommy Skinner and Phil Sparkes. The *Western Mail & Echo*-sponsored Taff Swim was first held in the River Taff in 1924 but moved to Roath Park Lake in 1931. *(Western Mail & Echo)*

Welsh actress Ruth Madoc and Father Christmas (Samuel Bradbury) are surrounded by shoppers in Allders, *c.* 1983. *(Marilyn Collard)*

Carpet fitters and seamstresses from David Morgan family store and their children at the annual works sports day at Ely Paper Mills grounds, *c.* 1957. *(D. Piper)*

Before the last war, the crowning of the May Queen used to be held in the castle grounds. This picture shows the 1932 May Queen Barbara Davies. The picture's donor Mrs Audrey Davies (née Martin) also took part in the proceedings. *(Mrs Audrey Davies)*

The Donovan and Edmunds family at the Nazareth House fête held at Blackweir Fields. The ladies, from left to right, are Karen Sorenson, Eileen Sorenson, Mary Donovan, Ann Donovan, Elaine Edmunds, Eileen Donovan and Elsie Donovan. The men, from left to right, are Walter Donovan and Cyril Edmunds, *c.* 1956. *(Philip Donovan)*

The inaugural meeting of the new, and short-lived, 1973–96 South Glamorgan County Council authority took place in the City Hall and to celebrate the occasion thirty-eight Conservative councillors and forty-two Labour councillors posed for the picture. *(John Smith)*

10

Leisure Time

This picture, taken at Cardiff Arms Park in June 1973, shows the young ladies who used to parade the greyhounds before the start of each race. Carole Ellery (née Norman) and Leslie Coles are second and fourth from the right respectively. The first girl on the right was called Jane, an art student who lived in Cyncoed. The donor of the picture is Pat Harding holding the number 3 dog. *(Pat Harding)*

Trainer Fred Goodman (left) walking Pride of Tudor, and owner Malcolm Davies with Lillyput Queen at greyhound kennels St Mellons near Cardiff, 1977. *(Malcolm Davies)*

Cardiff butcher Malcolm Davies being congratulated after his Lillyput Queen had won the last greyhound race to be held at the Cardiff Arms Park on 31 July 1977. *(Malcolm Davies)*

Kennel lass Beatrice Hodges poses for a picture supposedly with the legendary greyhound Mick the Miller, who won the 1930 Welsh Greyhound Derby at the Welsh White City Stadium in a world record time of 29.55 seconds for the standard distance of 525 yards, *c.* 1930. *(Donald Williams)*

Tom and Eileen Cronin (left) with greyhound trainer Paddy Cochlan and Pat Hegarty, daughter of the Cardiff Arms Park greyhound racing manager, at the greyhound racing company's annual dinner and dance, *c.* 1960. *(Tom Cronin)*

The Eastern Leisure Centre at Llanrumney which was formally opened by Mr James Callaghan MP in September 1982. *(Western Mail & Echo)*

Mr F. Oatten's party from Cardiff poses for a group picture outside the Abbey Mills Café, Gloucestershire, on 4 September 1937. *(Author's Collection)*

Schweppes staff charabanc outing, 26 July 1928. First on the left, wearing a headband, is Beatrice Hodges (see also page 102). The company were situated in Newport Road. *(Ronald Shackell)*

Schweppes staff outing in the 1920s. *(Donald Williams)*

Another Schweppes staff outing and Beatrice Hodges can be seen seated wearing her favourite headband, 1926. *(Donald Williams)*

Pub and work outings were very popular at one time and these ladies from the Criterion Hotel in Church Street seemed to be enjoying themselves on this occasion in the 1950s. *(Mrs Geraldine Huntley)*

Phyllis and Tony Blood, mine hosts of The Salutation which was situated on the corner of Hayes Bridge Road and Homfray Street, *c.* 1980. *(Tony Blood)*

The interior of The Salutation, which was first licensed in 1847. It closed in 1982, a couple of years after this picture is believed to have been taken. *(Tony Blood)*

Ira Stevens (standing) and her friend Audrey Lewis. In 1936 when she was five, Ira went to Hollywood and became the legendary child star Shirley Temple's double and stand-in. She appeared in *Little Princess* and other films and returned to Cardiff in 1939 when her work permit ran out, *c.* 1940. *(Audrey Hellier Leunt)*

The Cardiff Snowflakes Choir, established in 1926, entertained thousands of people for more than fifty years. Under their musical director, Miss Eira Novello Williams, they won many awards including the International award in 1947 and 1949 at Llangollen. Ira Stevens, who became a member, can be seen three rows from the top, third from the left, *c.* 1945. *(Audrey Hellier Leunt)*

Cardiff's popular Roath Park attracts well over a million visitors a year. It was opened in 1894 and this postcard picture was probably taken in the 1920s or early 1930s. *(Author's Collection)*

The Captain Robert Falcon Scott clock tower was erected in 1915 as a memorial to Scott's ill-fated 1910 Antarctic expedition, *c.* 1950. *(Author's Collection)*

When the lake first opened as many as 2,000 bathers could be found swimming there on Sunday mornings. Note the changing huts to the left of the picture. The lake was declared off limits to swimmers in the 1960s, *c.* 1928. *(Author's Collection)*

The islands at Roath Park lake, 1928. There are more than fifty species of waterfowl resident on the lake and the islands. *(Author's Collection)*

Three men in a boat! Roath Park has seen many changes since this postcard picture was taken in the 1920s. *(Author's Collection)*

A magnifying glass reveals that the boat was called *Britannia, c. 1920. (Ernest T. Bush)*

Visitors to Roath Park crowd around the bandstand to enjoy a concert, *c.* 1920. *(Author's Collection)*

This little boy appears to be more interested in the photographer than the concert, *c.* 1920. *(Author's Collection)*

The old bandstand in Grange Gardens, *c.* 1910. It was replaced many years later. *(Author's Collection)*

Gorsedd Gardens, Cathays Park, 1938. This attractive little park is situated in the civic centre. *(Author's Collection)*

Victoria Park, home of the legendary Billy the Seal. Before the last war the park had a small zoo, *c.* 1928. *(Author's Collection)*

The statue of the third Marquess of Bute, unveiled in 1930, is situated in Friary Gardens on Kingsway, *c.* 1950. *(Author's Collection)*

The scuplture 'Joyance' by William Goscombe John is the most famous feature of Thompson's Park and was installed in 1928. It is a replica of the original that was stolen. There is another replica at St Fagan's Castle. The park is named after Charles Thompson who presented it to the people of Cardiff in 1911. The author worked in the park as a young lad. These picture postcards were taken in about 1930. *(Author's Collection)*

Sophia Gardens, which was named after the Marchioness of Bute. She only visited the park on one occasion in her lifetime, *c. 1950. (Author's Collection)*

The old Central Library in Trinity Street, *c.* 1904. It opened in 1892 and was replaced by a new library at St David's Link in 1987. Ironically, the new library was demolished in 2007 but there are plans for the old library to become Cardiff's Local History Museum. *(Author's Collection)*

The foundation stone for the National Museum of Wales was laid in 1912 but owing to the First World War the main block and western galleries were not completed until 1927. This picture was taken in the 1960s. *(Gerald May)*

For many years, Cardiffians have made the short trip to Barry Island by bus, train and car to enjoy the delights of the seaside, 1953. *(Author's Collection)*

We do like to be beside the seaside! Barry Island promenade, 1955. *(Author's Collection)*

A popular attraction in Barry Island was the Figure 8 Railway which was constructed in 1912. It was replaced in 1939 by the Scenic Railway, *c. 1913. (Author's Collection)*

The ladies and gentlemen's bathing houses, built in 1905, have long since been demolished, *c. 1913. (Author's Collection)*

This view of the bathing pool at Barry Island was taken from Friar's Point, *c. 1930*. *(Author's Collection)*

For peace and quiet, Cardiffians still visit the pebble beach at Porthkerry, Coldnap, Barry, *c. 1927*. *(Author's Collection)*

11
Cardiff at War

British troops await the order to disembark the SS *Rangitiki* at Cardiff Docks,
16 October 1942. (*Associated British Ports*)

Vehicles being discharged from the Sea Train *Texas*, Cardiff Docks, March 1944. *(Associated British Ports)*

Midship section of a tank landing craft being discharged by floating crane at Cardiff Docks, 19 October 1942. *(Associated British Ports)*

The American troopship *Santa Paula* gets ready to leave Cardiff Docks, 18 November 1943. Built in 1932, she could hold 2,200 passengers and was one of the most active transport ships of the Second World War making twenty-eight overseas voyages in four years. *(Associated British Ports)*

Hundreds of small boats like these seen in the Queens Dock in October 1946 took part in the evacuation of British troops from Dunkirk. The ship in the right-hand corner of the picture is the *Fort Poplar* of London. *(Associated British Ports)*

King George VI (extreme right), Queen Elizabeth (only the top of her hat can be seen between the two gentlemen looking towards the camera) and Princess Elizabeth (centre) visited Cardiff Docks in March 1941. *(Associated British Ports)*

Many women were employed in Cardiff Docks during the Second World War, *c.* 1945. *(Associated British Ports)*

St David's Roman Catholic Cathedral in Charles Street was gutted by incendiary bombs in 1941. The cathedral, built in 1887, was later rebuilt on the same site in 1959. *(Author's Collection)*

Neville Street, Riverside, where seven people in one house died during a bombing raid on 2 January 1941. *(Western Mail & Echo)*

The damaged interior of Llandaff Cathedral which was also bombed in January 1941. A landmine reduced the cathedral to a shell and many of the Victorian wood carvings were destroyed. *(Western Mail & Echo)*

The houses numbered 33 to 43 in St Agnes Road, Heath, were destroyed in a bombing raid on the city in 1943. *(Author's Collection)*

Houses in Prospect Drive, Fairwater, were also destroyed in a bombing raid during the Second World War. *(Western Mail & Echo)*

Cardiff Docks was also bombed during the Second World War and this picture shows damage to the Crown Fuel Company premises gantry, engine house and stables in February 1941. (*Associated British Ports*)

During the Second World War, thousands of Cardiffians were supplied with Anderson air-raid shelters like this one in the garden of a house in Pearl Street in Splott, *c.* 1945. (*Author's Collection*)

To celebrate the end of the war Astrid and David Mouncher, of Mynachdy Road in Gabalfa, took part in a VJ Day fancy dress competition, 1945. *(David Mouncher)*

All the fancy dress competitors lined up for this group picture, 1945. *(David Mouncher)*

After war celebrations at Mynachdy Road. All the children seem to be enjoying themselves, 1945. *(David Mouncher)*

More celebrations, this time at Pengam Street in Tremorfa, and the looks on the children's faces says it all, 1945. *(D. Harding)*

12

Happiest Days
of their Lives!

Fireman Sam (Derek Carder) collecting money for charity soon had the attention of
these schoolchildren on the corner of Working Street and St John's Street, 1989.
(Derek Carder)

Infants of Marlborough Road School, Roath, *c.* 1938. *(Wendy Huggett)*

Children of Marlborough Road School posed for this group picture in the 1930s. *(Wendy Huggett)*

Smiles all round! These Marlborough Road School pupils look so happy. The girl with the pigtails and white bows is Wendy Huggett, *c. 1940.* (*Wendy Huggett*)

One wonders what became of these Marlborough Road School pupils, *c. 1938.* (*Wendy Huggett*)

Judging by their outfits these Marlborough Road School pupils were in a school play, *c.* 1935. *(Wendy Huggett)*

Only two of these pupils of St Illtyd's College are pictured wearing their caps, *c.* 1944. *(Wendy Huggett)*

Graham and Andrew Piper with Father Christmas at David Morgan's family store, December 1960. *(D. Piper)*

A children's Christmas party at David Morgan's family store in 1960. *(D. Piper)*

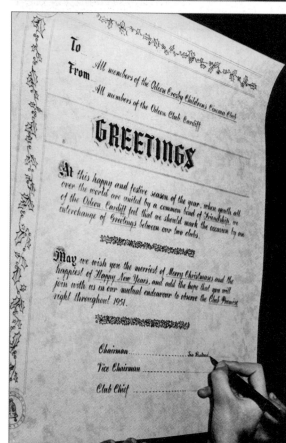

Mr Ian Craig, manager of the Odeon Cinema in Queen Street, watching David Mouncher signing the greetings certificate (left) which was sent to members of the Odeon Cinema Club in Crosby, 1950. (*David Mouncher*)

The daughter of Mr Craig gives the greetings scroll to the pilot at Tremorfa (Cardiff) Airport, 1951. From left to right are David Mouncher, Graem Batterscombe, Conway and Chrissie Stellars, all members of the Odeon Saturday Morning Children's Cinema Club. *(David Mouncher)*

David Mouncher and Shirley Bushard (on the right), with other members of the Odeon Cinema Club celebrating Crab Apple day, 1951. *(David Mouncher)*

Cardiff ex-British heavyweight champion Jack Petersen shows his Lonsdale belt to members of the Odeon Cinema Club, *c. 1950. (David Mouncher)*

The 19th Cub Pack at their meeting place in Arthur Street, 2 January 1944.
The lad not wearing a uniform is Gordon H. Gray who later become custodian of Cardiff Castle and lived there for more than ten years. *(Gordon H. Gray)*

Kevin Keenoy and his sister Maeve (aged six) outside the Globe Cinema in 1982. Eight-year-old Kevin presented a 1,151 signature petition opposing the closure of the cinema to the City Council's Mike Walker and although the cinema had a reprieve it was eventually closed in 1985 and demolished soon after. *(Western Mail & Echo)*

Allensbank Road Infants School, 1939. *(Ray Evans)*

Pupils of St Patrick's Roman Catholic School, Grangetown, *c.* 1930. (*Mary Cowan*)

St Joseph's Roman Catholic School, Heath, 1953. Some of the pupils in this picture are Andy Thomson, Frank Milton, Paul Colley, John Williams, Michael Martin, Peter Good, Michael Healan, Paul Horrigan, Bernard Poyser, Peter Macey, Christopher Rose, Desmond Vick, Michael Coughlan, Richard Hartley-Davies, Rosalie Wilks, Annette Evans, Veronica Elliott and Elizabeth Doyle. (*Andy Thomson*)

Patricia McDonald, aged twelve, in traditional Welsh dress advertising the national daily newspaper of Wales the *Western Mail*. The picture was probably taken to celebrate St David's Day, 1938. *(Mary Cowan)*

Pupils of Splottlands Secondary Modern School in 1948. Schoolteacher Mr Prosser is on the left of the picture. *(John James)*

Group picture of 4th Cardiff Scout Troup taken at Cardiff General railway station as they wait for a train to Cornwall, August 1951. *(Colin Merrick)*

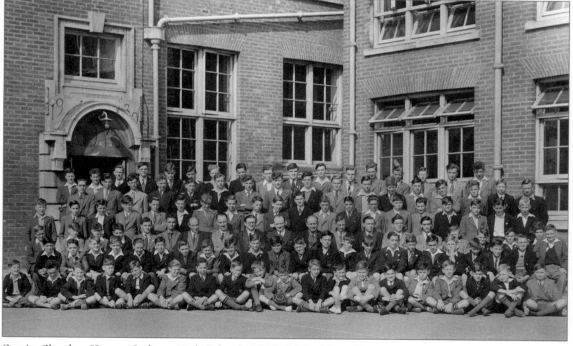

Owain Glyndwr House, Cathays High School, 1950. *(Colin Merrick)*

13

Sporting Moments

Maindy Stadium was built on the site of Maindy Pool which had claimed the lives of a number of people – adults and children – over the years. It was said to be 85ft deep and this picture shows workmen searching for the body of a little girl on 27 August 1928. *(Author's Collection)*

Workmen laying the Maindy Stadium running track in 1950. Cathays High School can be seen in the background. *(Author's Collection)*

The stadium was opened in 1951 and the cycle track was one of the best in the world at that time. 1953. *(Author's Collection)*

Stones from the filled-in Glamorgan Canal were used to build the terraces, seen here in 1950. Sadly, only the cycle track currently remains. (*Author's Collection*)

Cyclists race before a packed grandstand on 14 August 1957. (*Author's Collection*)

Welsh International athlete Ron Jones wins the first heat of the men's 100 yards at the 1968 Welsh AAA Senior Championships. He went on to win the final clocking 9.7 seconds. Between 1959 and 1970 he won the title eight times. *(Clive Phillips)*

Welsh junior sprint champion Clive Phillips (left) wins the most exciting and closest finish of the 1955 track season. He pipped Tony Carnes (Barry Grammar School) to win the Welsh AAA Junior 4x110 yards relay for Roath (Cardiff) Harriers. He went on to become a leading sports journalist with the *Western Mail & Echo. (Clive Phillips)*

Arguably Wales's greatest athlete, long jumper Lynn Davies prepares the sandpit before his epic battle with the American world record holder Ralph Boston at the 1965 Welsh Games. *(Clive Phillips)*

Ming Campbell (on the far left of the picture), later to become leader of the Liberal Democrat Party, is involved in a close finish with Lynn Davies, in the number 2 shirt, at the 1964 Welsh Games, Maindy Stadium. *(Clive Phillips)*

Author Brian Lee (left) who captained the *Western Mail & Echo* team in 1982 which won the Business Houses Relay Race at Pontcanna Fields, receives the trophy from Gordon Mcilroy of Les Croupiers as managing director Howard Green looks on. The other winning team members were Lee Beames, Malcolm Farnham and Rodney Savage. *(Western Mail & Echo)*

Above: The halfway stage in the 1982 *Western Mail* Marathon and author Brian Lee (number 32) fails to grab a drink. Despite his gaunt appearance, he went on to complete the course in just over three hours. *(Western Mail & Echo)*

One of the best British heavyweight boxers was Cardiff's Jack Petersen (1911–90), seen here during sparring practice, *c.* 1930. *(Author's Collection)*

Cathays
High School
Junior XV,
1949/50.
(*Colin
Merrick*)

Cardiff Ladies Hockey Club, 1952. Standing third from the left is Ray Evans (née Thomas). Some of the others in the picture are Judy Zeidman, Sonia Davies, Sheila Williams and Betty Soames (captain). *(Mrs Ray Evans)*

The Grange Albion baseball team which beat St Francis in the 1964 Silver Bowl final at Maindy Stadium on 30 July 1964. Names include John Furnham, Jimmy Gee, ? Burnett, Peter Kane, ? Duffield, Ted Pearse, Terry O'Grady, George Payne, Ken Taylor, Peter Duffin (captain), Paddy Gee, Gil Reece and Michael Gee.

The start of the Taff Swim which was held in Roath Park Lake between 1931 and 1961. It was first held in the River Taff in 1924. This picture was probably taken in the 1950s. *(Author's Collection)*

SECOND DAY

OFFICIAL
PROGRAMME.

PRICE
6D.

S. H. Wilton Pye

CARDIFF RACES

(UNDER NATIONAL HUNT RULES)

MONDAY AND TUESDAY,
APRIL 10TH AND 11TH, 1939

Patrons.

THE MARQUESS OF BUTE.   THE VISCOUNT TREDEGAR.
THE EARL OF PLYMOUTH.   LORD GLANELY.
THE MACKINTOSH OF MACKINTOSH.

Stewards.

LORD GLANELY.   ROBERT H. WILLIAMS, Esq.
C. C. WILLIAMS, Esq.,   THE VISCOUNT PORTMAN, M.F.H.

Officials.

Handicapper : Mr. R. TURNER.   *Starter :* Mr. F. WILLIAMS.
Judge : Mr. JOHN COVENTRY.
Auctioneer : Mr. A. WILKINSON.
Clerk of the Scales : Mr. FRANK WOOD.
Club Secretary : Major S. B. WILDMAN, O.B.E., 5, High Street, Cardiff.
Medical Officers :
Dr. FREDERICK WILLIAM CAMPBELL, Physician and Surgeon, West Orchard, Llandaff.
Dr. G. E. LINDSAY, "Westcross," Penarth.
Veterinary Surgeons :
Mr. JOHN LORD PERRY, M.R.C.V.S., 58, Newport Road, Cardiff.
Mr. JAMES HAMILTON STEWART, M.R.C.V.S., 14, Neville Street, Cardiff.
Clerk of the Course and Stakeholder : Mr. T. H. WILTON PYE, Broad Street Chambers, 32, Broad Street, Worcester.

Prices (Including Tax).

Course, 2/- ; Public Stand, 5/- ; Tattersalls : Gentlemen 12/6
Ladies 6/-.
Motors, 2/6 each, NOT including Occupants.

Western Mail & Echo Ltd., Cardiff.—2664r.

Official race card for Cardiff Races, 11 April 1939. Horseracing took place at Cardiff's Ely Racecourse from 1855 until 1939. *(Author's Collection)*

The old grandstand, Ely Racecourse. As many as 40,000 race-goers attended Ely Racecourse in the late 1890s at the time this picture was taken. *(Author's Collection)*

From left to right are famous Welsh jockey Evan Williams, his father Fred Williams the popular starter, Mrs Aubrey Hastings and Tommy Wilton-Pye the Clerk of the Course, *c.* 1930. *(Author's Collection)*

A day at the races! Dr Mona C. Davies, Mr Elystan Bowen Davies and Mrs Catherine Bowen Davies at Ely Racecourse, *c.* 1930. *(Author's Collection)*

The water jump at Ely Racecourse. 'The most important Welsh racecourse is at Ely, a suburb of Cardiff. It is left-handed with a circumference of just over 1 mile 3 furlongs, the first mile of which is perfectly straight.' No 42 in the Lucana cigarette Famous Racecourse series, *c.* 1925. *(Harry Welchman)*

Members of Cardiff Race Club enjoying a day at Ely races, 28 April 1937. *(Mary Clay)*

Local jockey David Thomas who won the 1926 Welsh Grand National at Ely Racecourse on Miss Balscadden. *(Author's Collection)*

Harry Llewellyn, later Sir Harry, of show-jumper Foxhunter fame, is led in after winning the Llanrumney Handicap Steeplechase on China Sea, who was completing a four-timer, at Ely Racecourse in November 1937. *(Author's Collection)*

Opposite, top: David Thomas leads the field on the eventual winner Miss Balscadden (number 22) in the 1926 Welsh Grand National. Miss Balscadden won the race again in 1928 with Welsh jockey George Bowden in the saddle. *(Author's Collection)*

Opposite, bottom: Over the sticks at Ely Racecourse, 26 May 1927. *(Mary Clay)*

In 1958 Cardiff hosted the sixth British Empire and Commonwealth Games. The track and field events took place at the famous Cardiff Arms Park. *(Author's Collection)*

The opening ceremony of the sixth British Empire and Commonwealth Games, Cardiff Arms Park. *(Author's Collection)*